The Adventures of Stampy Cat

A Minecraft Novel Based on StampyLongNose (Part 1)

Minecraft Game Writers &

Captainsparklez

LEGAL & DISCLAIMER

TABLE OF CONTENTS

DEDICATION

This Minecraft book is dedicated to all the Minecraft fans out there.

This is a work of fan fiction created *by fans, for fans*.

We hope you enjoy this short and enjoyable story!

If you do enjoy this book, please leave a review as we would love to hear from our fans.

Thanks and enjoy!

PART 1

The sun rose and shined through the window. Stampy squinted at the bright light and turned away.

BUZZ BUZZ BUZZ

Stampy's alarm went off and he jumped out of bed with a yelp. The alarm read 7:00am. It was time for Stampy to get ready and get to work.

Today was a special day for Stampy Cat. Today he was going to go on a very, very special adventure with a few of his best pals.

Stampy grabbed his telephone and dialed his best friend, Squiddy.

"Squiddy, my friend! Are you ready for our adventure?"

"Hey Stampy! Of course I am. I've been so excited I haven't gone to sleep. I ate a lot of candy and ice cream last night and I just could not fall asleep. WOO!"

Squiddy was clearly very excited for today.

"Okay, chap! That's great. Get ready and meet me at my house in 1 hour."

"Sounds good, Stampy! See you then. I shall bring you some

ice cream... Oh wait never mind. I don't have any left. I seem to have eaten all of it last night."

Stampy hung up the phone and ran to the bathroom. He washed his face and his golden fur.

"Looking good!" Stampy said as he smiled at himself in the mirror. He was one foxy cat.

He grabbed some gel and smoothed out his fur. One little piece of fur was being stubborn.

Stampy hissed at the cowlick in the mirror. He kept trying to push it down, but it kept popping up. It was one stubborn piece of fur.

Stampy reached in his drawer for some extra strength hair goop. He grabbed a big blob and rubbed it between his paws.

Unfortunately for Stampty, he had never used the super hair goop before. So when Stampy rubbed it between his paws, he realized something quite important...

His paws were quite furry. The goop got stuck between his fur and his fingers got stuck together! Stampy could not move his hands.

Each time he struggled, it would only get worse.

"UGH!" Stampy cried out in frustration.

He rolled on the floor, twisting and turning, but it was no use. In fact, things just kept getting worse.

Stampy stumbled into his shower cubicle and used his tail to turn on the water. He reached for a bar of soap but it kept slipping and sliding.

Finally, after about 5 minutes of struggles, Stampy got the soap into his hands.

He rubbed the soap on his hands, the best he could before the soap slipped and fell on the floor

"That's good enough..." Stampy said, fed up. He put his hands semi-soapy hands under the water.

The water splashed all over Stampy. His well groomed hair, minus the cowlick, got soaked with water. Stampy jumped in shock when the cold water hit his body.

He jumped so high his paws got stuck to the ceiling! Soapy as they were, the goo was much stronger. It overpowered the soap and Stampy got stuck to the ceiling.

He was hanging by his paws, dangling over the soapy shower floor.

Stampy's eyes popped out of his head!

"AHHH!" He shouted.

Then suddenly, his phone began to ring.

RING RING, RING RING
When Stampy couldn't get to the phone, the voicemail picked up.

"Hey Stampy, it's me! I'll be over in 5 minutes. See you soon buddy!"

It was Squiddy!

"Oh no, Squiddy's almost here!" Stampy panicked.

He quickly started to think. He looked around for anything that could help. There was nothing!

Then, he had an idea. Stampy started to swing. Side to side he swung. He could feel the goo loosening. He was going to fall on the floor. Good things cats always land on their....

BAM!

Stampy hit the floor. His face smashed into the drain.

"Ouch..." Stampy whined, slowly getting up. As he began to stand, he slipped on the bar of soap and fell on his bottom.

"AH!" Stampy squeaked. It was not a good morning!

Then, there was a knocking at the door. Stampy put all his strength together and used his tail to help him stand.

He pushed his way out of the bathroom and then he was faced with another dilemma. He had to unlock the front door and let his friend inside.

Sadly, his hands were still stuck together. Stampy would have to think outside the box.

He went to the window and tried to get Squiddy's attention. He waves around, but it was of no use. Squiddy was too distracted checking his map to notice Stampy's movement in the window.

"Squiddy!" Stampty shouted.

Finally Squiddy turned towards the noise and saw Stampy in the window.

"Hey Stampy! Let me in!" Squiddy shouted!

Right when Stampy was about to tell Squiddy what happened... Stampy accident tripped over his coffee table. He stubbed his toe and fell to the floor.

He hissed in pain and little tears came out from the corner of his eyes.

"Stampy!" Squiddy shouted, still locked outside the front door.

Stampy was in so much pain that he just lay on the floor for a few minutes. He looked lifeless.

Squiddy went and peeked through the window. He saw some blood on the floor from Stampy's injury.

"Stampy!" He shouted, worried.

When Stampy didn't move or respond, Sqiuddy started to panic. He was terrified that Stampy was knocked out... Or worse, dead!

Squiddy started to panic. He paced back and forth on Stampy's front porch.

Squiddy decided he should call their friend, Barry. He whipped out his cell phone and dialed their friend Barry the bear.

"Barry! Stampy's bleeding and he won't move or talk... I think he's...."

Within 5 seconds, Barry was there.

"How did you get here so fast?" Squiddy asked.

"I live next door, Squiddy..." Barry said, shaking his head at Squiddy.

"Oh... Right..." Squiddy replied shyly.

"Okay, so what happened here?"

"Well, we were supposed to go.. do some things today." Squiddy said suspiciously, "So I told Stampy I'd be over in like an hour. When I got here, he was acting all weird. He wouldn't let me in and then he was being all loud and then he ended up on the floor like... that."

Barry looked at Squiddy with a blank look. Squiddy was known to be the silly and confused one in their little group.

Barry began to investigate and then he started to put his own version of the story together.

He looked through the window with his glasses and noticed the blood on the floor was coming from Stampy's foot.

He noticed that Stampy's fur was very ruffles and messy. That was very strange because Stampy always looked his best, especially when he knew he had company coming over.

He then noticed something that explained everything! Barry noticed Stampy's cowlick!

Barry started laughing. He giggled and giggled until he was on the floor clutching his tummy.

"HAHHAHAHAHHAAHA"

"Barry! How could you be laughing at this situation? Our best friend could be... dead!"

Barry walked back to his house and quickly came back with something shiny in his hand. It was a spare key to Stampy's place.

"You had a key this whole time...?" Squiddy asked looking at Barry with disdain.

"Yep. HAHA" Barry laughed and walked in.

Squiddy rushed to Stampy's side. He threw his head onto Stampy's back to listen for a heartbeat.

"Um... Wrong side, buddy..." Barry said.

"Oh right!" Squiddy replied before flipping Stampy over.

"Hssssssss" Stampy hissed.

"You're alive buddy!" Squiddy said excitedly, squeezing poor Stampy with all his might.

"You're...Crushing...Me"

"Oh sorry, buddy! What happened?" Squiddy asked.

"It's a long story...." Stampy sighed. He still couldn't move much. On top of having his paws stuck, his whole body was aching.

"Let me guess." Barry interrupted, "You had some problem with your fur and you used the super strength goop you borrowed from me a while ago."

"Yeah..." Stampy said with a guilty expression. He had

borrowed Barry's super goo a long time ago, but he never gave it back.

Barry started laughing and rolling on the floor.

"What's so funny?" Squiddy and Stampy asked together.

"It's a long story..." Barry said, still laughing.

"No, I want to know!!!" Stampy said, "You're being suspicious!"

"Hahahhahahahahaokay! Fine i'll tell you..."

"Well remember how you borrowed that goop from me a long time ago? Well... After I asked you for it, you still didn't give it back..." Barry said sadly, "So one day I came up with a plan. I snuck into your house..." Barry could not contain his giggles.

"Sorry, so like I was saying," He continued, "So I snuck into your house using the spare key you gave me and I swapped out my goo for super glue...." He really could not contain his laughed now! Barry burst out in tears, "So... When you used it... It would be... Stuck to you! Hahahahahah!"

Stampy looked at Barry with very angry eyes.

"Uh oh." Squiddy said as he watched the two from behind the couch.

"You... Messed... With... My Hair..." Stampy said sternly..

"Oh c'mon. It was just a joke. No harm, no foul." Barry responded shrugging his shoulders.

"No harm? Do you see this?!" Stampy shouted while sticking his sore red toe in front of Barry's face.

"Oh that's nothing! You know how many cowlicks I had to go through because you wouldn't give me my goo back?" Barry cried out.

"Barry..." Squiddy tried to interrupt.

"Not now Squiddy!" Barry and Stampy said at once.

"Guys, listen...." Squiddy tried again, but it was no use.

"Be quiet, Squiddy. This is between me and him!" Stampy said.

Squiddy got upset and sat in the corner quietly.

"Because of you, I couldn't move my paws! I got stuck to the ceiling, fell down and hurt myself. So there was a lot of harm in this buddy. If you wanted the goo so bad why didn't you just buy some!" Stampy shouted with his face in Barry's face.

"Okay fine... I'm sorry... But that goo is super hard to find. They don't just sell it anywhere... It takes a lot of work to make. It need a lot of rare ingredients...."

"Oh well.." Stampy tried to think of something else to yell at Barry about, but he had an epiphany. There was no use arguing. The best solution was to work together, "I'm sorry, Barry. I shouldn't have taken your goo in the first place. How about we go on a quest and get all the ingredients and make more goo?"

"That sounds... Nice..." Barry said.

"Guys!" Squiddy cried with all his might.

"What's up Squiddy?" Stampy asked.

"Is this what you're looking for?"

Squiddy held up a glowing tub of super strength goo.

"I found it under the couch..." Squiddy said.

"Wait, if that's the goo.. What have you been using, Barry?" Stampy asked.

"I don't know...." Barry said. His eyes bulged with confusion.

A few minutes later, the doorbell rang. It was Mary Bear, Barry's wife.

"Hey guys. I'm off to the store, do you need anything?" She asked.

"No we're good Mary, thanks!" The boys replied.

"Is that my super strength goo?" Mary said, spotting the container in Squiddy's hands.

"Oh yeah that's Barry's hair gel." Stampy said.

"That's not for your fur..." Mary said slowly, "It's for furniture."

The boys stared at Mary with blank looks on their face. They just all started laughing. Confused, Mary finally asked, "What's so funny?"

"It's a long story, honey." Barry laughed.

"Alright well I'll see you boys later. Don't get in too much trouble now!"

"Bye Mary!" The boys shouted in unison.

So for the last few months, Stampy's hair goo was actually

super glue. Originally, the goo he borrowed from Barry was actually furniture goo to fix broken things. But what had Barry been using all this time?

After the boys said there goodbyes, Barry went home and checked for his goo. It was gone. He was so tired from all the craziness that he just decided to hibernate for the next few weeks.

Meanwhile, Squiddy was walking home. While passing by Barry's house, he saw a tub of goo on the floor. It was glowing. He picked it up and walked home humming a song.

The boys realized something today. At the end of the day, sharing and honesty is the best way to go.

Stampy would never over borrow again! Barry would never try to trick his friends with dangerous products.. And well Squiddy... Squiddy would just be Squiddy.

The End.

PART 2

COMING SOON

Made in the USA
Lexington, KY
24 August 2014